Little Pebble™

Bodies of Water

Rivers

A 4D BOOK

by Erika L. Shores

PEBBLE
a capstone imprint

Download the Capstone 4D app!

- Ask an adult to download the Capstone 4D app.
- Scan the cover and stars inside the book for additional content.

When you scan a spread, you'll find fun extra stuff to go with this book! You can also find these things on the web at www.capstone4D.com using the password: rivers.14681

Little Pebble is published by Pebble
1710 Roe Crest Drive, North Mankato,
Minnesota 56003
www.mycapstone.com

Library of Congress Cataloging-in-Publication Data
Library of Congress Cataloging-in-Publication Data is available on the Library of Congress website.
ISBN: 978-1-5435-1468-1 (library binding) —
978-1-5435-1472-8 (paperback) —
978-1-5435-1476-6 (ebook PDF)

Editorial Credits
Bobbie Nuytten, designer; Morgan Walters, media researcher; Tori Abraham, production specialist

Photo Credits
Shutterstock: Kokhanchikov, 11, Massimo Cattaneo, 7, Menno Schaefer, 19, Ohmayzing, 13, Phonix_a Pk.sarote, 21, Piotr Piatrouski, 5, Proskurina Yuliya, (wave) design element throughout, Scott Pooley, 17, Thabo Sibeko, 9, Therese Hansen, 15, Xiong Wei, Cover, 1

Printed and bound in China.
000309

Table of Contents

What Is a River?

A river is a moving

body of water.

Rivers twist. Rivers turn.

Rivers start in mountains
or tall hills.
The start is called
the source.

Where a river ends
is called the mouth.

mouth

Rivers flow into
lakes, other rivers,
or oceans.

What Is in a River?

Trees and plants grow
by rivers.
Where it's cold,
pine trees grow.

In warm places,
tall grasses grow.

Crocodiles swim

in the warm Nile River.

Splash!

Salmon are fish.

They live in cold rivers.

People and Rivers

Boats travel on rivers.

People catch fish.

Glossary

crocodile—a large, scaly reptile with short legs and strong jaws

mountain—a very tall piece of land, higher than a hill

mouth—the place where a stream or river enters a larger body of water

salmon—a large fish with silvery skin

source—the place where a river begins

Read More

Bang, Molly, and Penny Chisholm. *Rivers of Sunlight: How the Sun Moves Water Around the Earth.* New York: The Blue Sky Press, 2016.

Fishman, Jon M. *The Salmon's Journey.* Amazing Migrators. Minneapolis: Lerner Publications, 2018.

Flores, Mina. *Lakes, Rivers, and Streams.* Spotlight on Earth Science. New York: PowerKids Press, 2017.

Internet Sites

Use FactHound to find Internet sites related to this book.

Visit www.facthound.com

Just type in 9781543514681 and go

Check out projects, games and lots more at
www.capstonekids.com

Critical Thinking Questions

1. What is the place called where a river starts?

2. Describe crocodiles. Use the photo on page 17 and the glossary to help you.

3. What grows along rivers?

Index